Even though the number of birthdays I've had technically qualifies me as an adult, I see some caps here that I'd love to have. I guess "grown ups" will have to settle for the joys of crocheting one of these caps for a special kid…or kids. If you find yourself with a cap collection too large to be worn by the children in your world, even if they wore more than one at a time, check out local charities. To find a great match for your handmade gift, you can search the web using the words "charity crochet" and your city. Take a minute to find the perfect hat for that special kid, yours or someone else's, and get started. You can always find kids in need of the warmth and care that only a gift made with love can provide. I'd love to hear about it. Send me a note at KnitCrochetEditor@leisurearts.com.

Cheryl

Cheryl Johnson
Knit & Crochet
Publication Director

P.S. if you'd like to find out more about what's happening at Leisure Arts and the projects I have in the works, visit my blog at http://livinginamaterialworld.blogspot.com.

no adults ALLOWED!

Sweetness personified.
Loves a challenge.
Irrepressibly unique.
A laugh a minute.

Remind you of the captivating kiddos you know? Just imagine them enjoying these fifteen crocheted chill-chasers by designer Kay Meadors! The sizes for the caps and hats vary, so you'll find the perfect pattern for each young person, from preemie baby to active teen. There's also a blanket for wee ones and a scarf with cloche set for preteens.

Want to find more fun designs for kids? Visit ***www.leisurearts.com*** to browse our extensive library of instruction books and DVDs.

I0892828

LEISURE ARTS, INC
little rock, ar

INTERMEDIATE

Finished Size: 35" x $41^{1}/_{2}$"
(89 cm x 105.5 cm)

MATERIALS
Medium Weight Yarn (MEDIUM 4)
Version A
(6 ounces, 312 yards
(170 grams, 285 meters)
per skein):
Green - 2 skeins
Blue - 2 skeins
Off-White - 1 skein
Version B
(3 ounces, 165 yards
(85 grams, 151 meters) per
skein):
Lavender - 5 skeins
Yellow - 2 skeins
($2^{1}/_{2}$ ounces, 130 yards
(70 grams, 119 meters) per
skein):
Variegated - 4 skeins

Crochet hook,
size H (5 mm) **or** size
needed for gauge
Yarn needle

GAUGE SWATCH:
$6^{1}/_{2}$" (16.5 cm) square
Work same as Motif.

baby's favorite BLANKIE

STITCH GUIDE

BEGINNING CLUSTER (uses first 3 dc)
Ch 2, ★ YO, insert hook in **next** dc, YO and pull up a loop, YO and draw through 2 loops on hook; repeat from ★ once **more**, YO and draw through all 3 loops on hook.

CORNER CLUSTER (uses one sp)
★ YO, insert hook in sp indicated, YO and pull up a loop, YO and draw through 2 loops on hook; repeat from ★ 2 times **more**, YO and draw through all 4 loops on hook.

CLUSTER (uses next 3 dc)
★ YO, insert hook in **next** dc, YO and pull up a loop, YO and draw through 2 loops on hook; repeat from ★ 2 times **more**, YO and draw through all 4 loops on hook.

VERSION A - COLOR SEQUENCE

Rnds 1 and 2: Off-White
Rnds 3 and 4: Blue
Rnds 5 and 6: Green

VERSION B - COLOR SEQUENCE

Rnds 1 and 2: Yellow
Rnds 3 and 4: Variegated
Rnds 5 and 6: Lavender

MOTIF (Make 30)

With color indicated, ch 4; join with slip st to form a ring.

Rnd 1 (Right side)**:** Ch 3 **(counts as first dc, now and throughout)**, 2 dc in ring, ch 3, (3 dc in ring, ch 3) 3 times; join with slip st to first dc: 12 dc and 4 ch-3 sps.

Note: Loop a short piece of yarn around any stitch to mark Rnd 1 as **right** side.

Rnd 2: Work Beginning Cluster, ch 2, work (Corner Cluster, ch 3, Corner Cluster) in next corner ch-3 sp, ch 2, ★ work Cluster, ch 2, work (Corner Cluster, ch 3, Corner Cluster) in next corner ch-3 sp, ch 2; repeat from ★ 2 times **more**; join with slip st to top of Beginning Cluster, finish off: 12 Clusters and 12 sps.

Rnd 3: With **right** side facing, join next color with slip st in any corner ch-3 sp; ch 3, (2 dc, ch 2, 3 dc) in same sp, 3 dc in each of next 2 ch-2 sps, ★ (3 dc, ch 2, 3 dc) in next corner ch-3 sp, 3 dc in each of next 2 ch-2 sps; repeat from ★ 2 times **more**; join with slip st to first dc: 48 dc and 4 ch-2 sps.

Instructions continued on page 6.

INTERMEDIATE

Finished Size: 17" (43 cm) head circumference

MATERIALS
Medium Weight Yarn (MEDIUM 4)
(6 ounces, 330 yards (170 grams, 302 meters) per skein):
- Dark Blue - 1 skein
- Lt Blue - 1 skein
- White - 1 skein

Crochet hook, size H (5 mm) **or** size needed for gauge
Yarn needle

GAUGE: 15 sc and 16 rows = 4" (10 cm)

Gauge Swatch: 4" (10 cm) square
With Dark Blue, ch 16.
Row 1: Sc in second ch from hook and in each ch across: 15 sc.
Rows 2-16: Ch 1, turn; sc in each sc across.
Finish off.

make waves HAT

STITCH GUIDE

2-SC DECREASE (uses next 2 sts)
Pull up a loop in next 2 sc, YO and draw through all 3 loops on hook **(counts as one sc)**.

3-SC DECREASE (uses next 3 sts)
Pull up a loop in next 3 sc, YO and draw through all 4 loops on hook **(counts as one sc)**.

2-DC DECREASE (uses next 2 sts)
★ YO, insert hook in **next** st, YO and pull up a loop, YO and draw through 2 loops on hook; repeat from ★ once **more**, YO and draw through all 3 loops on hook **(counts as one dc)**.

3-DC DECREASE (uses next 3 sts)
★ YO, insert hook in **next** st, YO and pull up a loop, YO and draw through 2 loops on hook; repeat from ★ 2 times **more**, YO and draw through all 4 loops on hook **(counts as one dc)**.

RIBBING

With Dark Blue, ch 6.

Row 1: Sc in second ch from hook and in each ch across: 5 sc.

Row 2 (Right side)**:** Ch 1, turn; sc in Back Loop Only of each sc across *(Fig. 5, page 33)*.

Note: Loop a short piece of yarn around any stitch to mark Row 2 as **right** side.

Rows 3-62: Ch 1, turn; sc in Back Loop Only of each sc across.

Do **not** finish off.

BODY

Row 1: Ch 1, do **not** turn; working in end of rows, 2 sc in first row, sc in next row and in each row across: 63 sc.

Row 2: Ch 1, turn; sc in each sc across.

Instructions continued on page 7.

baby's favorite BLANKIE

Instructions continued from page 2.

Rnd 4: Ch 1, sc in same st and in next 2 dc, 3 sc in next corner ch-2 sp, sc in next dc and in each dc around working 3 sc in each corner ch-2 sp; join with slip st to first sc, finish off: 60 sc.

Rnd 5: With **right** side facing, join next color with slip st in center sc of any corner 3-sc group; ch 3, (dc, ch 2, 2 dc) in same st, dc in next sc and in each sc around to center sc of next corner 3-sc group, ★ (2 dc, ch 2, 2 dc) in center sc, dc in next sc and in each sc around to center sc of next corner 3-sc group; repeat from ★ 2 times **more**; join with slip st to first dc: 72 dc and 4 ch-2 sps.

Rnd 6: Ch 1, sc in same st and in next dc, 3 sc in next corner ch-2 sp, sc in next dc and in each dc around working 3 sc in each corner ch-2 sp; join with slip st to first sc, finish off: 84 sc.

FINISHING

Using Green (Version A) or Lavender (Version B), whipstitch Motifs together ***(Fig. 9, page 34)***, beginning in center sc of first corner and ending in center sc of next corner, forming 5 vertical strips of 6 Motifs each; then whipstitch strips together in same manner.

EDGING

Rnd 1: With **right** side facing, join Blue (Version A) **or** Lavender (Version B) with slip st in any corner sc; ch 3, (dc, ch 2, 2 dc) in same st, ★ † dc in next 20 sc, 2 dc in each of next 2 sc (same sc as seam) †; repeat from † to † across to last Motif on side, dc in next 20 sc, (2 dc, ch 2, 2 dc) in next corner sc; repeat from ★ 2 times **more**, then repeat from † to † across to last Motif, dc in last 20 sc; join with slip st to first dc: 528 dc and 4 ch-2 sps.

Rnd 2: Ch 1, sc in same st and in next dc, 3 sc in next corner ch-2 sp, sc in next dc and in each dc around working 3 sc in each corner ch-2 sp; join with slip st to first sc, finish off: 540 sc.

Rnd 3: With **right** side facing, join Green (Version A) **or** Variegated (Version B) with slip st in any corner sc; ch 1, working from **left** to **right**, skip next sc, ★ work reverse sc in next sc ***(Figs. 8a-d, page 34)***, ch 1, skip next sc; repeat from ★ around; join with slip st to first st, finish off.

make waves HAT

Instructions continued from page 4.

Row 3: Ch 1, turn; sc in each sc across changing to Lt Blue in last sc made ***(Fig. 6, page 33)***; cut Dark Blue.

Row 4: Ch 1, turn; sc in first 2 sc, hdc in next sc, dc in next sc, 3 dc in next sc, dc in next sc, hdc in next sc, ★ sc in next sc, hdc in next sc, dc in next sc, 3 dc in next sc, dc in next sc, hdc in next sc; repeat from ★ across to last 2 sc, sc in last 2 sc changing to White in last sc made, do **not** cut Lt Blue: 83 sts.

Row 5: Ch 1, turn; sc in first sc, work 2-sc decrease, sc in next 2 sts, 3 sc in next dc, sc in next 2 sts, ★ work 3-sc decrease, sc in next 2 sts, 3 sc in next dc, sc in next 2 sts; repeat from ★ across to last 3 sts, work 2-sc decrease, sc in last sc.

Row 6: Ch 1, turn; sc in first sc, work 2-sc decrease, sc in next 2 sc, 3 sc in next sc, sc in next 2 sc, ★ work 3-sc decrease, sc in next 2 sc, 3 sc in next sc, sc in next 2 sc; repeat from ★ across to last 3 sc, work 2-sc decrease, sc in last sc changing to Lt Blue; cut White.

Row 7: Ch 3 **(counts as first dc)**, turn; work 2-dc decrease, dc in next sc, hdc in next sc, sc in next sc, hdc in next sc, dc in next sc, ★ work 3-dc decrease, dc in next sc, hdc in next sc, sc in next sc, hdc in next sc, dc in next sc; repeat from ★ across to last 3 sc, work 2-dc decrease, dc in last sc changing to Dark Blue, cut Lt Blue: 63 sts.

Rows 8-16: Ch 1, turn; sc in each st across.

Row 17: Ch 1, turn; sc in first 7 sc, work 2-sc decrease, (sc in next 7 sc, work 2-sc decrease) across: 56 sc.

Row 18: Ch 1, turn; sc in first 6 sc, work 2-sc decrease, (sc in next 6 sc, work 2-sc decrease) across: 49 sc.

Row 19: Ch 1, turn; sc in first 5 sc, work 2-sc decrease, (sc in next 5 sc, work 2-sc decrease) across: 42 sc.

Row 20: Ch 1, turn; sc in first 4 sc, work 2-sc decrease, (sc in next 4 sc, work 2-sc decrease) across: 35 sc.

Row 21: Ch 1, turn; sc in first 3 sc, work 2-sc decrease, (sc in next 3 sc, work 2-sc decrease) across: 28 sc.

Row 22: Ch 1, turn; sc in first 2 sc, work 2-sc decrease, (sc in next 2 sc, work 2-sc decrease) across: 21 sc.

Row 23: Ch 1, turn; sc in first sc, work 2-sc decrease, (sc in next sc, work 2-sc decrease) across: 14 sc.

Row 24: Ch 1, turn; work 2-sc decrease across; finish off leaving a long end for sewing: 7 sc.

Thread yarn needle with long end and weave through remaining 7 sc; pull **tightly** to close. With **wrong** side and ends of rows together, sew back seam.

INTERMEDIATE

Finished Size: 11" (28 cm) head circumference

MATERIALS

Medium Weight Yarn (MEDIUM 4)
(6 ounces, 330 yards (170 grams, 302 meters) per skein):
Yellow - 1 skein
(5 ounces, 260 yards (140 grams, 238 meters) per skein):
Variegated - 1 skein
Crochet hook, size H (5 mm) **or** size needed for gauge
Yarn needle

GAUGE: Rnds 1-6 of Crown = 3³/₄" (9.5 cm);
15 sc = 4" (10 cm)

Gauge Swatch: 4" (10 cm) diameter

Rnd 1: With Yellow, ch 2, 7 sc in second ch from hook; join with slip st to first sc.

Rnd 2: Ch 1, 2 sc in same st and in each sc around; join with slip st to first sc: 14 sc.

Rnds 3-6: Work same as Rnds 2-5 of Crown: 42 sc.

Finish off.

birthday CAKE CAP

STITCH GUIDE

BACK POST SINGLE CROCHET *(abbreviated BPsc)*

Insert hook from **back** to **front** around post of st indicated *(Fig. 7, page 33)*, YO and pull up a loop, YO and draw through both loops on hook.

DECREASE (uses next 2 sc)

Pull up a loop in next 2 sc, YO and draw through all 3 loops on hook **(counts as one sc)**.

CURLICUES

Rnd 1 (Right side)**:** With Variegated, ch 2, 7 sc in second ch from hook; join with slip st to Front Loop Only of first sc ***(Fig. 5, page 33)***.

Note: Loop a short piece of yarn around any stitch to mark Rnd 1 as **right** side.

Rnd 2: Ch 8, slip st in second ch from hook, (ch 1, slip st in next ch) 6 times, ★ slip st in Front Loop Only of next sc, ch 8, slip st in second ch from hook, (ch 1, slip st in next ch) 6 times; repeat from ★ 5 times **more**; join with slip st to free loop of first sc on Rnd 1 ***(Fig. 4a, page 33)***, do **not** finish off: 7 Curlicues.

CROWN

Rnd 1: Ch 1, working in free loops of sc on Rnd 1, 2 sc in same st and in each sc around; join with slip st to first sc: 14 sc.

Rnd 2: Ch 1, sc in same st, 2 sc in next sc, (sc in next sc, 2 sc in next sc) around; join with slip st to first sc: 21 sc.

Rnd 3: Ch 1, sc in same st and in next sc, 2 sc in next sc, (sc in next 2 sc, 2 sc in next sc) around; join with slip st to first sc: 28 sc.

Rnd 4: Ch 1, sc in same st and in next 2 sc, 2 sc in next sc, (sc in next 3 sc, 2 sc in next sc) around; join with slip st to first sc: 35 sc.

Rnd 5: Ch 1, sc in same st and in next 3 sc, 2 sc in next sc, (sc in next 4 sc, 2 sc in next sc) around; join with slip st to first sc: 42 sc.

Rnd 6: Ch 2 **(counts as first hdc)**, hdc in next sc and in each sc around; join with slip st to first hdc, finish off.

BODY

Rnd 1: With **right** side facing and inserting hook from **back** to **front** around post of first hdc ***(Fig. 7, page 33)***, join Yellow with slip st; ch 1, work BPsc around same st and each hdc around; join with slip st to first BPsc.

Rnds 2-14: Ch 1, sc in same st and in each st around; join with slip st to first sc.

Rnd 15: Ch 1, sc in same st and in next 4 sc, 2 sc in next sc, (sc in next 5 sc, 2 sc in next sc) around; join with slip st to first sc: 49 sc.

Rnd 16: Ch 1, sc in same st and in next 4 sc, decrease, (sc in next 5 sc, decrease) around; join with slip st to first sc, finish off: 42 sc.

INTERMEDIATE

Finished Size: 11" (28 cm) head circumference

MATERIALS

Medium Weight Yarn (MEDIUM 4)
(6 ounces, 312 yards (170 grams, 285 meters) per skein):
Green - 1 skein
Blue - 1 skein
Crochet hook, size H (5 mm) **or** size needed for gauge
Yarn needle

GAUGE: 15 sc and 16 rows = 4" (10 cm)

Gauge Swatch: 4" (10 cm) square
With Green, ch 16.
Row 1: Sc in second ch from hook and in each ch across: 15 sc.
Rows 2-16: Ch 1, turn; sc in each sc across.
Finish off.

little guy preemie CAP

STITCH GUIDE

DECREASE (uses next 2 sc)
Pull up a loop in next 2 sc, YO and draw through all 3 loops on hook **(counts as one sc)**.

RIBBING

With Green, ch 5.

Row 1: Sc in second ch from hook and in each ch across: 4 sc.

Row 2 (Right side)**:** Ch 1, turn; sc in Back Loop Only of each sc across ***(Fig. 5, page 33)***.

Note: Loop a short piece of yarn around any stitch to mark Row 2 as **right** side.

Rows 3-42: Ch 1, turn; sc in Back Loop Only of each sc across.

Do **not** finish off.

BODY

Row 1: Ch 1, do **not** turn; sc in end of each row across: 42 sc.

Row 2: Ch 1, turn; sc in each sc across changing to Blue in last sc made ***(Fig. 6, page 33)***; do **not** cut Green.

Row 3: Ch 1, turn; sc in each sc across.

Row 4: Ch 1, turn; sc in each sc across changing to Green in last sc made; do **not** cut Blue.

Row 5: Ch 1, turn; sc in each sc across.

Rows 6-14: Repeat Rows 2-5 twice, then repeat Row 2 once **more**.

Row 15: Ch 1, turn; sc in first 4 sc, decrease, (sc in next 4 sc, decrease) across: 35 sc.

Row 16: Ch 1, turn; sc in first 3 sc, decrease, (sc in next 3 sc, decrease) across changing to Green in last sc made: 28 sc.

Row 17: Ch 1, turn; sc in first 2 sc, decrease, (sc in next 2 sc, decrease) across: 21 sc.

Row 18: Ch 1, turn; sc in first sc, decrease, (sc in next sc, decrease) across changing to Blue in last sc made: 14 sc.

Row 19: Ch 1, turn; decrease across: 7 sc.

Row 20: Ch 1, turn; sc in each sc across, do **not** change colors.

TOP LOOPS

Row 1: Ch 10, turn; slip st in Front Loop Only of first sc, ★ ch 10, slip st in Back Loop Only of next sc, ch 10, slip st in Front Loop Only of next sc; repeat from ★ across; finish off Blue only: 7 ch-10 loops.

Row 2: With **right** side facing and working in free loops of sc on Row 20 ***(Fig. 4a, page 33)***, insert hook in first sc and pull up a loop with Green, ★ ch 10, working in **front** of ch-10 on Row 1, slip st in free loop of next sc, ch 10, working **behind** ch-10 on Row 1, slip st in free loop of next sc; repeat from ★ across, finish off leaving a long end for sewing.

Thread yarn needle with long end and sew back seam and ends of Ribbing. Fold Ribbing up to form a brim and tack in place.

INTERMEDIATE

Finished Size:
Scarf - 5¼" x 73½" (13.5 cm x 186.5 cm)
Cloche - 21" (53.5 cm) head circumference

MATERIALS
Medium Weight Yarn (MEDIUM 4)
Version A
(5 ounces, 260 yards (141 grams, 238 meters) per skein**)**:
Tan - 1 skein
(6 ounces, 312 yards (170 grams, 285 meters) per skein**)**:
Black - 1 skein
Version B
(6 ounces, 312 yards (170 grams, 285 meters) per skein**)**:
Green - 1 skein
Orange - 1 skein
Red - 1 skein

Crochet hook, size I (5.5 mm) **or** size needed for gauge
Yarn needle

GAUGE SWATCH:
5¼" (13.5 cm) square
Work same as Motif.

your way scarf & cloche SET

STITCH GUIDE

BEGINNING CLUSTER (uses first 3 dc)
Ch 2, ★ YO, insert hook in **next** dc, YO and pull up a loop, YO and draw through 2 loops on hook; repeat from ★ once **more**, YO and draw through all 3 loops on hook.

CORNER CLUSTER (uses one sp)
★ YO, insert hook in sp indicated, YO and pull up a loop, YO and draw through 2 loops on hook; repeat from ★ 2 times **more**, YO and draw through all 4 loops on hook.

CLUSTER (uses next 3 dc)
★ YO, insert hook in **next** dc, YO and pull up a loop, YO and draw through 2 loops on hook; repeat from ★ 2 times **more**, YO and draw through all 4 loops on hook.

BEGINNING DECREASE (uses first 2 sc)
Pull up a loop in first 2 sc, YO and draw through all 3 loops on hook **(counts as one sc)**.

DECREASE (uses next 2 sc)
Pull up a loop in next 2 sc, YO and draw through all 3 loops on hook **(counts as one sc)**.

VERSION A - COLOR SEQUENCE
Rnds 1 and 2: Tan
Rnd 3: Black
Rnd 4: Tan

VERSION B - COLOR SEQUENCE
For Scarf - make 4 **each** of Motifs 1 and 2; make 3 **each** of Motifs 3 and 4
For Cloche - make 1 **each** of Motifs 1-4

	Motif 1	Motif 2	Motif 3	Motif 4
Rnds 1 & 2	Green	Red	Green	Orange
Rnd 3	Orange	Green	Red	Green
Rnd 4	Red	Orange	Orange	Red

Instructions begin on page 14.

ION A

VERSION B

SCARF

MOTIF (Make 14)

With color indicated, ch 4; join with slip st to form a ring.

Rnd 1 (Right side)**:** Ch 3 **(counts as first dc, now and throughout)**, 2 dc in ring, ch 3, (3 dc in ring, ch 3) 3 times; join with slip st to first dc: 12 dc and 4 ch-3 sps.

Note: Loop a short piece of yarn around any stitch to mark Rnd 1 as **right** side.

Rnd 2: Work Beginning Cluster, ch 2, work (Corner Cluster, ch 3, Corner Cluster) in next corner ch-3 sp, ch 2, ★ work Cluster, ch 2, work (Corner Cluster, ch 3, Corner Cluster) in next corner ch-3 sp, ch 2; repeat from ★ 2 times **more**; join with slip st to top of Beginning Cluster, finish off: 12 Clusters and 12 sps.

Rnd 3: With **right** side facing, join next color with slip st in any corner ch-3 sp; ch 3, (2 dc, ch 2, 3 dc) in same sp, 3 dc in each of next 2 ch-2 sps, ★ (3 dc, ch 2, 3 dc) in next corner ch-3 sp, 3 dc in each of next 2 ch-2 sps; repeat from ★ 2 times **more**; join with slip st to first dc, finish off: 48 dc and 4 ch-2 sps.

Rnd 4: With **right** side facing, join next color with sc any corner ch-2 sp ***(see Joining With Sc, page 33)***; 2 sc in same sp, sc in next dc and in each dc around working 3 sc in each corner ch-2 sp; join with slip st to first sc, finish off: 60 sc.

FINISHING

VERSION A

With Tan, whipstitch Motifs together *(Fig. 9, page 34)*, beginning in center sc on first corner and ending in center sc on next corner.

VERSION B

Arrange Motifs numerically, beginning with Motif 1 and ending with Motif 2. Using Red or Orange, whipstitch Motifs together *(Fig. 9, page 34)*, beginning in center sc on first corner and ending in center sc on next corner.

CLOCHE

MOTIF (Make 4)

Rnds 1-4: Following Color Sequence, page 12, work same as Scarf Motif, page 14: 60 sc.

JOINING

VERSION A

With Tan, whipstitch Motifs together to form a strip *(Fig. 9, page 34)*, beginning in center sc on first corner and ending in center sc on next corner, then whipstitch the first and last Motifs together to form a tube.

VERSION B

Arrange Motifs numerically, beginning with Motif 1 and ending with Motif 4. With Red or Orange, whipstitch Motifs together to form a strip *(Fig. 9, page 34)*, beginning in center sc on first corner and ending in center sc on next corner, then whipstitch Motifs 1 and 4 together to form a tube.

CROWN

Rnd 1: With **right** side facing, join Black (Version A) **or** Green (Version B) with sc in any center sc (same as seam); sc in next sc and in each sc around, working in center sc on each side of each seam; join with slip st to first sc: 64 sc.

Rnd 2: Ch 1, work beginning decrease, sc in next sc and in each sc around; join with slip st to first sc: 63 sc.

Rnd 3: Ch 1, sc in same st and in each sc around; join with slip st to first sc.

Rnd 4: Ch 1, sc in same st and in next 6 sc, decrease, (sc in next 7 sc, decrease) around; join with slip st to first sc: 56 sc.

Rnd 5: Ch 1, sc in same st and in next 5 sc, decrease, (sc in next 6 sc, decrease) around; join with slip st to first sc: 49 sc.

Rnd 6: Ch 1, sc in same st and in next 4 sc, decrease, (sc in next 5 sc, decrease) around; join with slip st to first sc: 42 sc.

Rnd 7: Ch 1, sc in same st and in next 3 sc, decrease, (sc in next 4 sc, decrease) around; join with slip st to first sc: 35 sc.

Rnd 8: Ch 1, sc in same st and in next 2 sc, decrease, (sc in next 3 sc, decrease) around; join with slip st to first sc: 28 sc.

Rnd 9: Ch 1, sc in same st and in next sc, decrease, (sc in next 2 sc, decrease) around; join with slip st to first sc: 21 sc.

Rnd 10: Ch 1, sc in same st, decrease, (sc in next sc, decrease) around; join with slip st to first sc: 14 sc.

Rnd 11: Ch 1, work beginning decrease, decrease around; join with slip st to first sc, finish off leaving a long end for sewing: 7 sc.

Thread yarn needle with long end and weave through remaining 7 sc; pull **tightly** to close and secure end.

BOTTOM EDGING

With **right** side facing, join same color as Crown with slip st in any sc; ch 1, working from **left** to **right**, work reverse sc in each sc around *(Figs. 8a-d, page 34)*; join with slip st to first st, finish off.

EASY

Finished Size: 14" (35.5 cm) head circumference

MATERIALS

Medium Weight Yarn (4 MEDIUM)
(4 ounces, 232 yards (113 grams, 212 meters) per skein):
- Variegated - 1 skein
- Green - 15 yards (13.5 meters)

Crochet hook, size I (5.5 mm) **or** size needed for gauge

Yarn needle

GAUGE: 14 sts and 8 rows = 4" (10 cm)

Gauge Swatch: 4" (10 cm) square

Ch 15.

Work same as Body Rows 1-8.

Finish off.

festive HAT

STITCH GUIDE

CROSS ST

(uses 2 ch-1 sps)

Dc in next ch-1 sp, working **around** dc just made, dc in same ch-1 sp as last Cross St made.

BODY

With Variegated, ch 50.

Row 1 (Wrong side)**:** Sc in second ch from hook and in each ch across: 49 sc.

Note: Loop a short piece of yarn around **back** of any sc on Row 1 to mark **right** side.

Row 2: Ch 4 **(counts as first dc plus ch 1)**, turn; skip next sc, dc in next sc, ★ ch 1, skip next sc, dc in next sc; repeat from ★ across: 25 dc and 24 ch-1 sps.

Row 3: Ch 3 **(counts as first dc)**, turn; skip first ch-1 sp, dc in next ch-1 sp, working **around** dc just made, dc in skipped ch-1 sp **(first Cross St made)**, work Cross St across to last dc, dc in last dc: 48 dc.

Row 4: Ch 1, turn; 2 sc in first dc, sc in next dc and in each dc across: 49 sc.

Rows 5-16: Repeat Rows 2-4, 4 times.

Finish off, leaving a long end for sewing.

FINISHING

Thread yarn needle with long end. With **wrong** side and ends of rows together, sew back seam.

TOP EDGING

With **right** side facing, join Green with slip st in first sc after seam; ch 1, (slip st in next sc, ch 1) around; join with slip st to first slip st, finish off.

BOTTOM EDGING

With **wrong** side facing and working in free loops of beginning ch ***(Fig. 4b, page 33)***, join Green with slip st in first ch after seam; ch 1, (slip st in next ch, ch 1) around; join with slip st to first slip st, finish off.

DRAWSTRING

With Green, make a Twisted Cord, 20" (51 cm) in length ***(see Twisted Cord, page 34)*** and weave it through ch-1 sps on Row 14. Pull Drawstring up to close top of Hat and tie in a bow.

Turn first four rounds up to form a brim.

INTERMEDIATE

Finished Size: 15" (38 cm) head circumference

MATERIALS

Medium Weight Yarn [MEDIUM 4]
(6 ounces, 312 yards (170 grams, 285 meters) per skein):
- Brown - 1 skein
- Tan - 15 yards (13.5 meters)

Crochet hook, size H (5 mm) **or** size needed for gauge

GAUGE SWATCH: 4" (10 cm) diameter
Work same as Rnds 1-7 of Crown.

l'il lumberjack CAP

STITCH GUIDE

BEGINNING DECREASE (uses first 2 sc)
Pull up a loop in first 2 sc, YO and draw through all 3 loops on hook **(counts as one sc)**.

DECREASE (uses next 2 sc)
Pull up a loop in next 2 sc, YO and draw through all 3 loops on hook **(counts as one sc)**.

CROWN

Rnd 1 (Right side)**:** With Brown, ch 2, 7 sc in second ch from hook; do **not** join, place marker to mark beginning of rnd ***(see Markers, page 33)***.

Note: Loop a short piece of yarn around any sc to mark Rnd 1 as **right** side.

Rnd 2: 2 Sc in each sc around: 14 sc.

Rnd 3: (Sc in next sc, 2 sc in next sc) around: 21 sc.

Rnd 4: (Sc in next 2 sc, 2 sc in next sc) around: 28 sc.

Rnd 5: (Sc in next 3 sc, 2 sc in next sc) around: 35 sc.

Rnd 6: (Sc in next 4 sc, 2 sc in next sc) around: 42 sc.

Rnd 7: (Sc in next 5 sc, 2 sc in next sc) around, do **not** finish off: 49 sc.

BODY

Rnds 1-13: Sc in each sc around.

LEFT FLAP

Row 1: Slip st in next sc, remove marker, ch 1, sc in same st and in next 9 sc: 10 sc.

Rows 2-8: Ch 1, turn; sc in each sc across.

Row 9: Ch 1, turn; work beginning decrease, sc in next 6 sc, decrease: 8 sc.

Row 10: Ch 1, turn; sc in each sc across.

Row 11: Ch 1, turn; work beginning decrease, sc in next 4 sc, decrease: 6 sc.

Rows 12 and 13: Ch 1, turn; sc in each sc across.

Finish off.

RIGHT FLAP

Row 1: With **right** side facing, skip 15 sc from Left Flap and join Brown with sc in next sc ***(see Joining With Sc, page 33)***; sc in next 9 sc, leave remaining sc unworked: 10 sc.

Rows 2-13: Work same as Left Flap; at end of Row 13, do **not** finish off: 6 sc.

EDGING

Rnd 1: Ch 1, do **not** turn; working in end of rows, skip first row, sc in next 12 rows, skip next sc, sc in next 12 sc, † skip next sc, sc in next 12 rows, skip last row, 2 sc in next sc, sc in next 2 sc, place marker in last sc made for st placement, sc in next 2 sc, 2 sc in next sc †, skip first row, sc in next 12 rows, skip next sc, sc in next 13 sc, repeat from † to † once; join with slip st to first sc, finish off: 89 sc.

Rnd 2: With **right** side facing, join Tan with slip st in same st as joining; ch 1, working from **left** to **right**, work reverse sc in next sc and in each sc across to first marked sc ***(Figs. 8a-d, page 34)***, † ch 25, working in back ridge of chs ***(Fig. 3, page 33)***, slip st in each ch across (Tie made), skip marked sc †, work reverse sc in next sc and in each sc across to next marked sc, repeat from † to † once, work reverse sc in next sc and in each sc around; join with slip st to first st, finish off.

EASY

Finished Size: 15¾" (40 cm) head circumference

MATERIALS
- Medium Weight Yarn (MEDIUM 4) (3 ounces, 153 yards (90 grams, 140 meters) per skein): 1 skein
- Crochet hook, size I (5.5 mm) **or** size needed for gauge
- Yarn needle

GAUGE: In pattern, 14 sts and 6 rows = 4" (10 cm)

Gauge Swatch: 4" (10 cm) square
Ch 16.
Work same as Body Rows 1-6.
Finish off.

easy breezy HAT

BODY

Ch 57.

Row 1: Dc in fourth ch from hook **(3 skipped chs count as first dc)** and in each ch across: 55 dc.

Row 2 (Right side)**:** Ch 4 **(counts as first dc plus ch 1, now and throughout)**, turn; skip next dc, dc in next dc, ★ ch 1, skip next dc, dc in next dc; repeat from ★ across: 28 dc and 27 ch-1 sps.

Note: Loop a short piece of yarn around any stitch to mark Row 2 as **right** side.

Row 3: Ch 3 **(counts as first dc, now and throughout)**, turn; dc in next ch-1 sp and in each dc and ch-1 sp across: 55 dc.

Row 4: Ch 4, turn; skip next dc, dc in next dc, ★ ch 1, skip next dc, dc in next dc; repeat from ★ across: 28 dc and 27 ch-1 sps.

Row 5: Ch 3, turn; dc in next ch-1 sp and in each dc and each ch-1 sp across: 55 dc.

Row 6: Ch 3, turn; dc in next dc and in each dc across.

Rows 7-15: Repeat Rows 4 and 5, 4 times; then repeat Row 4 once **more**: 28 dc and 27 ch-1 sps.

Finish off, leaving a long end for sewing.

FINISHING

Thread yarn needle with long end. With **wrong** side and ends of rows together, sew back seam. Turn first three rows up to form a brim and tack in place.

DRAWSTRING

Make a Twisted Cord, 24" (61 cm) long ***(see Twisted Cord, page 34)***. Weave Drawstring through ch-1 sps on Row 15; pull it up to close top of Hat. Tie in a bow.

OSHKOSH

EASY

Finished Size: 16" (40.5 cm) head circumference

MATERIALS

Medium Weight Yarn (MEDIUM 4)
(3 1/2 ounces, 196 yards (100 grams, 179 meters) per skein):
Variegated - 1 skein
White - 15 yards (13.5 meters)
Crochet hook, size G (4 mm) **or** size needed for gauge
Yarn needle

GAUGE: In pattern, 17 sts and 13 rows = 4" (10 cm)

Gauge Swatch: 4" (10 cm) square
With Variegated, ch 18.
Work same as Body for 13 rows.
Finish off.

tied up topper

BODY

With Variegated, ch 68.

Row 1 (Wrong side)**:** Sc in second ch from hook, ★ ch 1, skip next ch, sc in next ch; repeat from ★ across: 34 sc and 33 ch-1 sps.

Note: Loop a short piece of yarn around **back** of any stitch on Row 1 to mark **right** side.

Row 2: Ch 1, turn; sc in first sc and in next ch-1 sp, ★ ch 1, skip next sc, sc in next ch-1 sp; repeat from ★ across to last sc, sc in last sc: 35 sc and 32 ch-1 sps.

Row 3: Ch 1, turn; sc in first sc, ch 1, ★ skip next sc, sc in next ch-1 sp, ch 1; repeat from ★ across to last 2 sc, skip next sc, sc in last sc: 34 sc and 33 ch-1 sps.

Repeat Rows 2 and 3 until Body measures 8" (20.5 cm) from beginning ch; at end of last row, finish off leaving a long end for sewing.

FINISHING

Thread yarn needle with long end. With **wrong** side and ends of rows together, whipstitch top of Cap closed ***(Fig. 9, page 34)***. Sew side seam.

TIE

With Off-White, make a Twisted Cord, 18" (45.5 cm) long ***(see Twisted Cord, page 34)***. Thread each end through one corner of top seam. Pull the two corners slightly together and tie Cord in a bow.

EDGING

With White, work Blanket Stitch around bottom edge of Hat ***(Figs. 1a & b)***.

Turn bottom edge of Hat up to form a brim.

BLANKET STITCH

Come up at 1; go in at 2, leaving a small loop. Come up again at 3 directly below 2 and in line with 1 while holding yarn under needle with thumb ***(Fig. 1a)***. Pull yarn through. Repeat around edge ***(Fig. 1b)***.

Fig. 1a

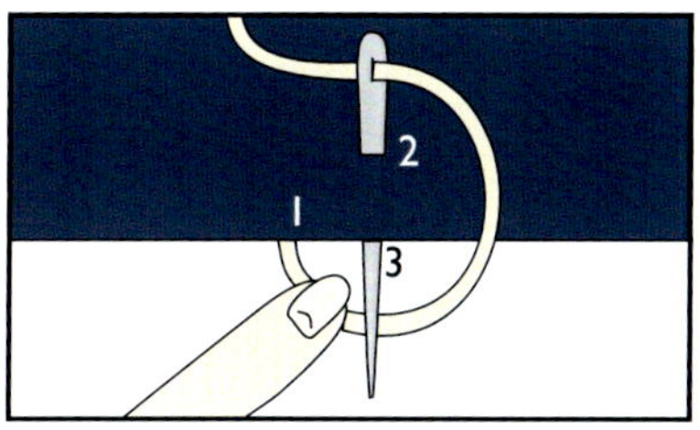

Fig. 1b

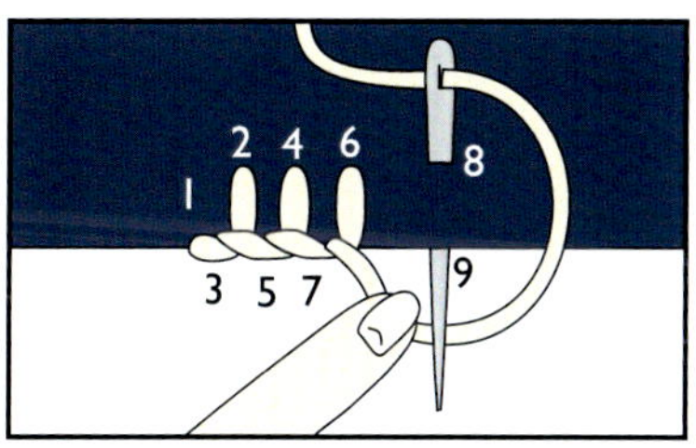

INTERMEDIATE

Finished Size: 17" (43 cm) head circumference

MATERIALS
- Medium Weight Yarn (MEDIUM 4) (3 ounces, 197 yards (85 grams, 180 meters) per skein):
  - Tan - 1 skein
  - Maroon - 1 skein
  - Green - 1 skein
  - Blue - 1 skein
- Crochet hook, size H (5 mm) **or** size needed for gauge
- Yarn needle
- Safety pin

GAUGE: In pattern,
15 sts = 4" (10 cm);
9 rows = 3³/₄" (9.5 cm)

Gauge Swatch: 4"w x 3³/₄"h (10 cm x 9.5 cm)
With Tan, ch 16.
Row 1: Sc in second ch from hook and in each ch across: 15 sc.
Rows 2-9: Work same as Body Rows 2-9.
Finish off.

tri corner CAP

STITCH GUIDE

FRONT POST SINGLE CROCHET *(abbreviated FPsc)*
Insert hook from **front** to **back** around post of dc indicated *(Fig. 7, page 33)*, YO and pull up a loop, YO and draw through both loops on hook. Skip st behind FPsc.

RIBBING

With Tan, ch 6.

Row 1: Sc in second ch from hook and in each ch across: 5 sc.

Row 2 (Right side)**:** Ch 1, turn; sc in Back Loop Only of each sc across *(Fig. 5, page 33)*.

Note: Loop a short piece of yarn around any stitch to mark Row 2 as **right** side.

Rows 3-62: Ch 1, turn; sc in Back Loop Only of each sc across.

Do **not** finish off.

BODY

Row 1: Ch 1, do **not** turn; working in end of rows, 2 sc in first row, sc in each row across: 63 sc.

Row 2: Ch 3 **(counts as first dc, now and throughout)**, turn; dc in next sc and in each sc across; slip loop from hook onto safety pin to keep piece from unraveling while you work the next row.

Row 3: With **right** side facing, join Maroon with slip st in first dc; (work FPsc around next dc, slip st in next dc) across; finish off Maroon.

Instructions continued on page 28.

INTERMEDIATE

Finished Size: 19¼" (49 cm) head circumference

MATERIALS

Medium Weight Yarn (MEDIUM 4)
(5 ounces, 260 yards (141 grams, 238 meters) per skein): 1 skein

Crochet hook, size H (5 mm) **or** size needed for gauge

Yarn needle

GAUGE: 15 dc and 7 rows = 4" (10 cm)

Gauge Swatch: 4" (10 cm) square

Ch 17.

Row 1: Dc in fourth ch from hook **(3 skipped chs count as first dc)** and in each ch across: 15 dc.

Rows 2-7: Ch 3 (counts as first dc), turn; dc in next dc and in each dc across.

Finish off.

elf CAP

STITCH GUIDE

DECREASE (uses next 2 dc)
★ YO, insert hook in **next** dc, YO and pull up a loop, YO and draw through 2 loops on hook; repeat from ★ once **more**, YO and draw through all 3 loops on hook **(counts as one dc)**.

RIBBING

Leaving a long end for sewing, ch 6.

Row 1: Sc in second ch from hook and in each ch across: 5 sc.

Row 2 (Right side)**:** Ch 1, turn; sc in Back Loop Only of each sc across ***(Fig. 5, page 33)***.

Note: Loop a short piece of yarn around any stitch to mark Row 2 as **right** side.

Rows 3-72: Ch 1, turn; sc in Back Loop Only of each sc across.

Do **not** finish off.

BODY

Rnd 1: Ch 1, do **not** turn; working in end of rows, sc in each row across; join with slip st to first sc: 72 sc.

Rnd 2: Ch 3 **(counts as first dc, now and throughout)**, dc in next sc and in each sc around; join with slip st to first dc.

Instructions continued on page 29.

tri corner CAP

Instructions continued from page 28.

Row 4: With **right** side facing, remove loop from safety pin and place on hook; ch 3, ★ dc in next FPsc, working **around** next slip st, dc in next dc on previous row; repeat from ★ across.

Row 5: Ch 3, turn; dc in next dc and in each dc across, slip loop from hook onto safety pin to keep piece from unraveling while you work the next row.

Row 6: With **right** side facing, join Green with slip st in first dc; (work FPsc around next dc, slip st in next dc) across; finish off Green.

Rows 7 and 8: Repeat Rows 4 and 5.

Row 9: With **right** side facing, join Blue with slip st in first dc; (work FPsc around next dc, slip st in next dc) across; finish off Blue.

Rows 10 and 11: Repeat Rows 4 and 5.

Rows 12-16: Repeat Rows 3-7.

Finish off leaving a long end for sewing.

FINISHING

Thread yarn needle with long end. With **wrong** side and ends of rows together, sew side seam.

Place markers in the 11th, 32nd, and 53rd stitch on Row 16.

Fold Row 16 in thirds with a marked st at each point. With Tan, whipstitch stitches of Row 16 together to form 3 corners of Cap ***(Fig. 9, page 34)***.

POM-POM (Make 1 each: Blue, Green, Maroon)

Cut a piece of cardboard 3" (7.5 cm) square. Wind the yarn around the cardboard until it is approximately 1/2" (12 mm) thick in the middle ***(Fig. 2a)***.

Carefully slip the yarn off the cardboard and firmly tie a 12" (30.5 cm) length of yarn around the middle ***(Fig. 2b)***. Leave yarn ends long enough to attach the pom-pom. Cut the loops on both ends and trim the pom-pom into a smooth ball ***(Fig. 2c)***.

Fig. 2a

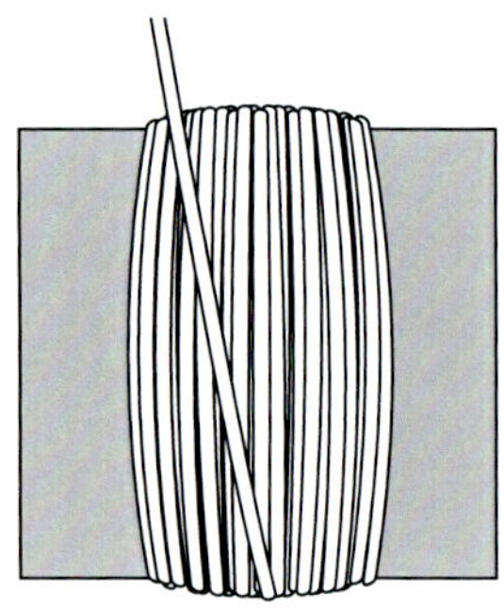

Fig. 2b

Fig. 2c

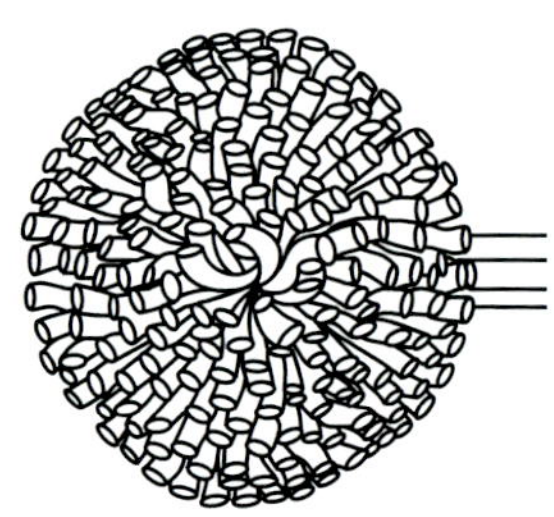

Attach a pom-pom to each corner of Cap.

elf CAP

Instructions continued from page 26.

Rnd 3: Ch 3, dc in next dc and in each dc around; join with slip st to first dc.

Rnd 4: Ch 3, dc in next 9 dc, decrease, (dc in next 10 dc, decrease) around; join with slip st to first dc: 66 dc.

Rnds 5 and 6: Ch 3, dc in next dc and in each dc around; join with slip st to first dc.

Rnd 7: Ch 3, dc in next 8 dc, decrease, (dc in next 9 dc, decrease) around; join with slip st to first dc: 60 dc.

Rnds 8 and 9: Ch 3, dc in next dc and in each dc around; join with slip st to first dc.

Rnd 10: Ch 3, dc in next 7 dc, decrease, (dc in next 8 dc, decrease) around; join with slip st to first dc: 54 dc.

Rnd 11: Ch 3, dc in next dc and in each dc around; join with slip st to first dc.

Rnd 12: Ch 3, dc in next 6 dc, decrease, (dc in next 7 dc, decrease) around; join with slip st to first dc: 48 dc.

Rnd 13: Ch 3, dc in next dc and in each dc around; join with slip st to first dc.

Rnd 14: Ch 3, dc in next 5 dc, decrease, (dc in next 6 dc, decrease) around; join with slip st to first dc: 42 dc.

Rnd 15: Ch 3, dc in next dc and in each dc around; join with slip st to first dc.

Rnd 16: Ch 3, dc in next 4 dc, decrease, (dc in next 5 dc, decrease) around; join with slip st to first dc: 36 dc.

Rnd 17: Ch 3, dc in next dc and in each dc around; join with slip st to first dc.

Rnd 18: Ch 3, dc in next 3 dc, decrease, (dc in next 4 dc, decrease) around; join with slip st to first dc: 30 dc.

Rnd 19: Ch 3, dc in next dc and in each dc around; join with slip st to first dc.

Rnd 20: Ch 3, dc in next 2 dc, decrease, (dc in next 3 dc, decrease) around; join with slip st to first dc: 24 dc.

Rnd 21: Ch 3, dc in next dc and in each dc around; join with slip st to first dc.

Rnd 22: Ch 3, dc in next dc, decrease, (dc in next 2 dc, decrease) around; join with slip st to first dc: 18 dc.

Rnd 23: Ch 3, dc in next dc and in each dc around; join with slip st to first dc.

Rnd 24: Ch 3, decrease, (dc in next dc, decrease) around; join with slip st to first dc: 12 dc.

Rnd 25: Ch 3, dc in next dc and in each dc around; join with slip st to first dc.

Rnd 26: Ch 2, dc in next dc, decrease around; skip beginning ch-2 and join with slip st to first dc: 6 dc.

Rnd 27: Ch 2, dc in next dc, decrease twice; skip beginning ch-2 and join with slip st to first dc, finish off: 3 dc.

FINISHING

Thread yarn needle with long end and sew Ribbing seam.

Make a 3¼" (8.5 cm) long Tassel ***(Figs. 10a & b, page 34)***.

Make a 12" (30.5 cm) long braid using 3 doubled strands of yarn. Attach one end of braid to Tassel and the other end to tip of Cap.

INTERMEDIATE

Finished Size: 19" (48.5 cm) head circumference

MATERIALS

Medium Weight Yarn (MEDIUM 4)
(6 ounces, 330 yards (170 grams, 302 meters) per skein):
- Black - 1 skein
- Grey - 1 skein
- Maroon - 1 skein

Crochet hook, size H (5 mm) **or** size needed for gauge
Yarn needle
Safety pin

GAUGE: In pattern, 15 sts and 11 rows = 4" (10 cm)

Gauge Swatch: 4" (10 cm) square
With Black, ch 16.
Row 1: Sc in second ch from hook and in each ch across: 15 sc.
Rows 2-11: Work same as Body Rows 2-11.
Finish off.

two tassels no hassles HAT

STITCH GUIDE

FRONT POST DOUBLE CROCHET *(abbreviated FPdc)*
YO, insert hook from **front** to **back** around post of st indicated *(Fig. 7, page 33)*, YO and pull up a loop (3 loops on hook), (YO and draw through 2 loops on hook) twice. Skip st behind FPdc.

RIBBING

With Black, ch 6.

Row 1: Sc in second ch from hook and in each ch across: 5 sc.

Row 2 (Right side)**:** Ch 1, turn; sc in Back Loop Only of each sc across *(Fig. 5, page 33)*.

Note: Loop a short piece of yarn around any stitch to mark Row 2 as **right** side.

Rows 3-70: Ch 1, turn; sc in Back Loop Only of each sc across.

Do **not** finish off.

BODY

Row 1: Ch 1, do **not** turn; working in end of rows, 2 sc in first row, sc in each row across: 71 sc.

Row 2: Ch 3 **(counts as first dc, now and throughout)**, turn; dc in next sc and in each sc across.

Row 3: Ch 3, turn; dc in next dc and in each dc across, slip loop from hook onto safety pin to keep piece from unraveling while you work the next row.

Row 4: With **right** side facing, join Grey with slip st in first dc; (work FPdc around dc one row below next dc, slip st in next dc) across; finish off Grey.

Row 5: With **right** side facing, remove loop from safety pin and place back on hook; ch 3, ★ dc in next FPdc, working **around** next slip st, dc in dc on previous row; repeat from ★ across.

Row 6: Ch 3, turn; dc in next dc and in each dc across, slip loop from hook onto safety pin to keep piece from unraveling while you work the next row.

Row 7: With **right** side facing, join Maroon with slip st in first dc; (work FPdc around dc one row **below** next dc, slip st in next dc) across; finish off Maroon.

Row 8: With **right** side facing, remove loop from safety pin and place back on hook; ch 3, ★ dc in next FPdc, working **around** next slip st, dc in dc on previous row; repeat from ★ across.

Rows 9-22: Repeat Rows 3-8 twice, then repeat Rows 3 and 4 once **more**.

Row 23: With **right** side facing, remove loop from safety pin and place back on hook; ch 1, working **around** first slip st, sc in dc on previous row, ★ sc in next sc, working **around** next slip st, sc in dc on previous row; repeat from ★ across.

Row 24: Ch 1, turn; sc in each sc across; finish off leaving a long end for sewing.

FINISHING

Thread yarn needle with long end. With **wrong** side and ends of rows together, whipstitch top seam *(Fig. 9, page 34)*. With Black, sew side seam.

TASSELS

Using all 3 colors, make two 4" (10 cm) long Tassels *(Figs. 10a & b, page 34)*.

Attach one Tassel to each corner of Hat.

general instructions

ABBREVIATIONS

BPsc	Back Post single crochet(s)
ch(s)	chain(s)
cm	centimeters
dc	double crochet(s)
FPsc	Front Post single crochet(s)
FPdc	Front Post double crochet(s)
hdc	half double crochet(s)
mm	millimeters
Rnd(s)	Round(s)
sc	single crochet(s)
sp(s)	space(s)
st(s)	stitch(es)
YO	yarn over

★ — work instructions following ★ as **many more** times as indicated in addition to the first time.

† to † — work all instructions from first † to second † **as many** times as specified.

( ) or **[ ]** — work enclosed instructions **as many** times as specified by the number immediately following **or** work all enclosed instructions in the stitch or space indicated **or** contains explanatory remarks.

colon (:) — the number(s) given after a colon at the end of a row or round denote(s) the number of stitches you should have on that row or round.

GAUGE

Exact gauge is **essential** for proper fit. Before beginning your project, make the sample swatch given in the individual instructions in the yarn and hook specified. After completing the swatch, measure it, counting your stitches and rows/rounds carefully. If your swatch is larger or smaller than specified, **make another, changing hook size to get the correct gauge**. Keep trying until you find the size hook that will give you the specified gauge.

CROCHET HOOKS	
Metric mm	**U.S.**
2.25	B-1
2.75	C-2
3.25	D-3
3.5	E-4
3.75	F-5
4	G-6
5	H-8
5.5	I-9
6	J-10
6.5	K-10½
9	N
10	P
15	Q

CROCHET TERMINOLOGY		
UNITED STATES		**INTERNATIONAL**
slip stitch (slip st)	=	single crochet (sc)
single crochet (sc)	=	double crochet (dc)
half double crochet (hdc)	=	half treble crochet (htr)
double crochet (dc)	=	treble crochet (tr)
treble crochet (tr)	=	double treble crochet (dtr)
double treble crochet (dtr)	=	triple treble crochet (ttr)
triple treble crochet (tr tr)	=	quadruple treble crochet (qtr)
skip	=	miss

Yarn Weight Symbol & Names	SUPER FINE 1	FINE 2	LIGHT 3	MEDIUM 4	BULKY 5	SUPER BULKY 6
Type of Yarns in Category	Sock, Fingering Baby	Sport, Baby	DK, Light Worsted	Worsted, Afghan, Aran	Chunky, Craft, Rug	Bulky, Roving
Crochet Gauge Ranges in Single Crochet to 4" (10 cm)	21-32 sts	16-20 sts	12-17 sts	11-14 sts	8-11 sts	5-9 sts
Advised Hook Size Range	B-1 to E-4	E-4 to 7	7 to I-9	I-9 to K-10.5	K-10.5 to M-13	M-13 and larger

BEGINNER	Projects for first-time crocheters using basic stitches. Minimal shaping.
EASY	Projects using yarn with basic stitches, repetitive stitch patterns, simple color changes, and simple shaping and finishing.
INTERMEDIATE	Projects using a variety of techniques, such as basic lace patterns or color patterns, mid-level shaping and finishing.
EXPERIENCED	Projects with intricate stitch patterns, techniques and dimension, such as non-repeating patterns, multi-color techniques, fine threads, small hooks, detailed shaping and refined finishing.

JOINING WITH SC

When instructed to join with sc, begin with a slip knot on hook. Insert hook in stitch or space indicated, YO and pull up a loop, YO and draw through both loops on hook.

MARKERS

Markers are used to help distinguish the beginning of each round being worked. Place a 2" (5 cm) scrap piece of yarn before the first stitch of each round, moving marker after each round is complete.

BACK RIDGE

Work only in loops indicated by arrows *(Fig. 3)*.

Fig. 3

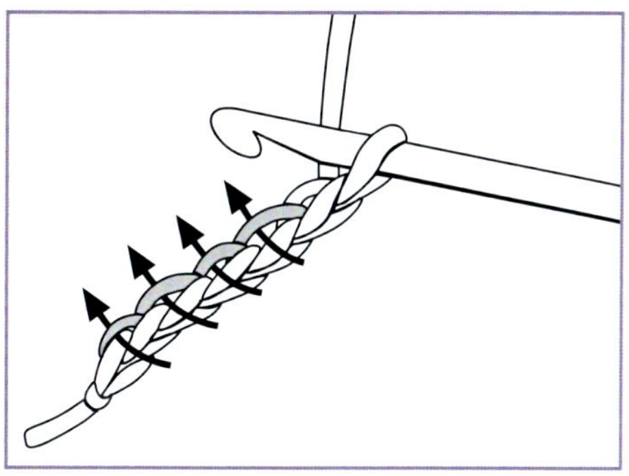

FREE LOOPS

After working in Back or Front Loops Only on a row or round, there will be a ridge of unused loops. These are called the free loops. Later, when instructed to work in the free loops of the same row or round, work in these loops *(Fig. 4a)*.
When instructed to work in free loops of a chain, work in loop indicated by arrow *(Fig. 4b)*.

Fig. 4a

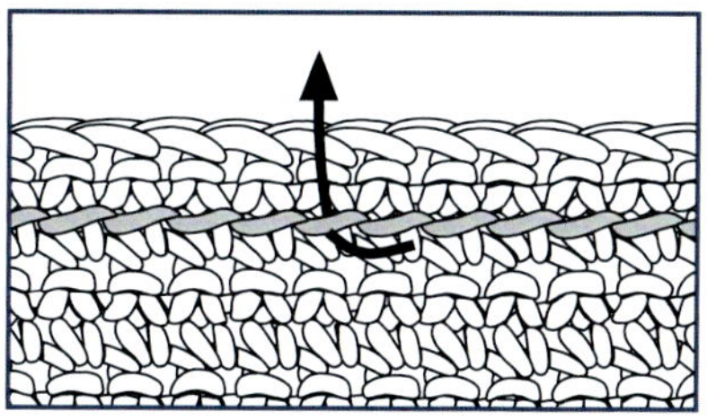

Fig. 4b

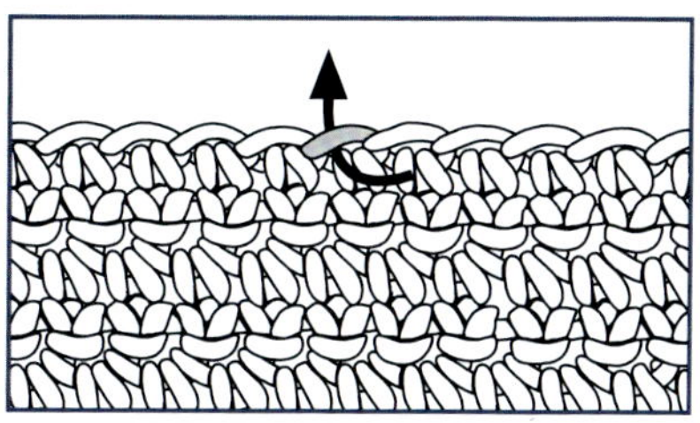

BACK OR FRONT LOOP ONLY

Work only in loop(s) indicated by arrow *(Fig. 5)*.

Fig. 5

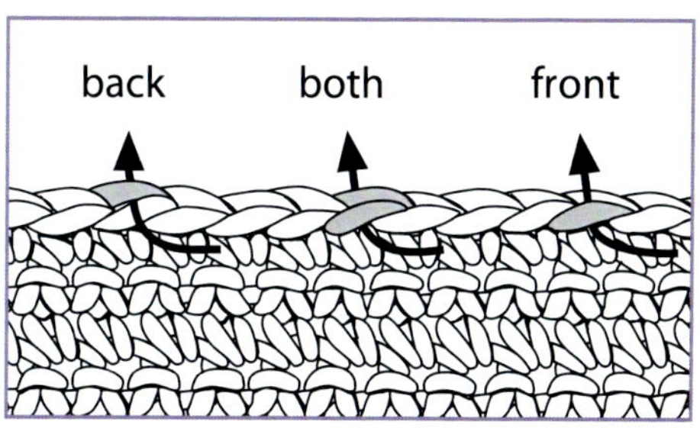

CHANGING COLORS

Work the last stitch to within one step of completion, hook new yarn *(Fig. 6)* and draw through all loops on hook. Carry yarn not being used loosely along edge of piece and do **not** cut yarn unless instructed.

Fig. 6

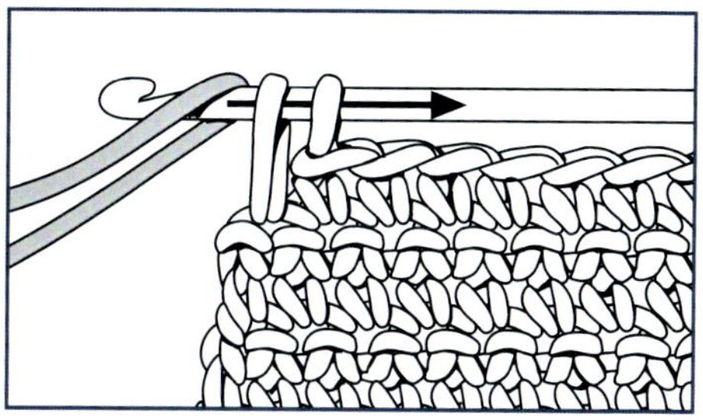

POST STITCH

Work around post of stitch indicated, inserting hook in direction of arrow *(Fig. 7)*.

Fig. 7

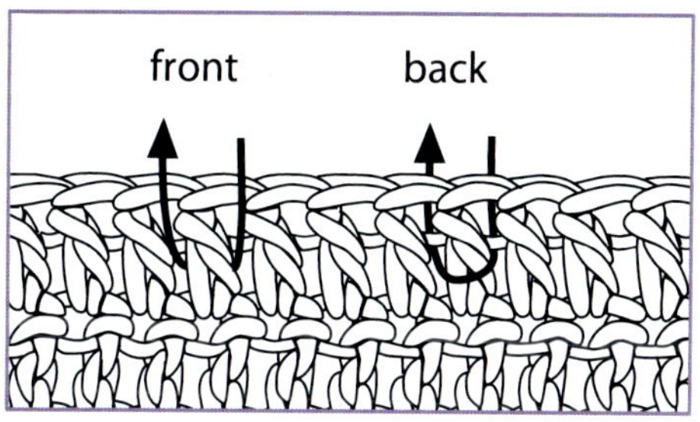

REVERSE SINGLE CROCHET

(abbreviated reverse sc)

Working from **left** to **right**, ★ insert hook in st to **right** of hook ***(Fig. 8a)***, YO and draw through, under and to **left** of loop on hook (2 loops on hook) ***(Fig. 8b)***, YO and draw through both loops on hook ***(Fig. 8c)*** **(reverse sc made, *Fig. 8d*)**; repeat from ★ around.

Fig. 8a

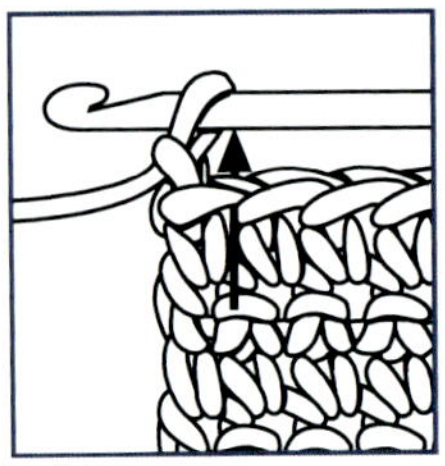

Fig. 8b

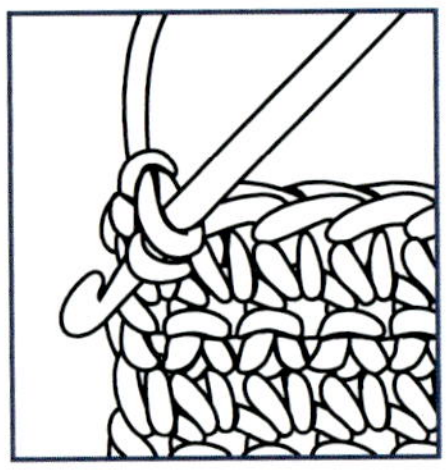

Fig. 8c

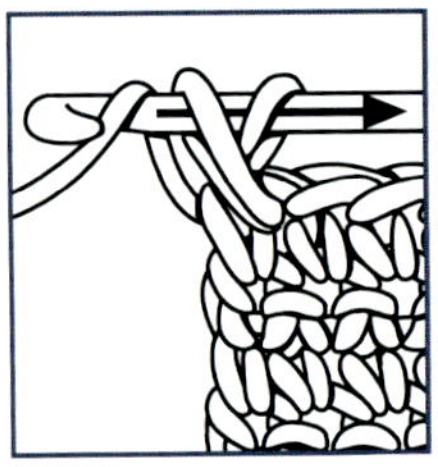

Fig. 8d

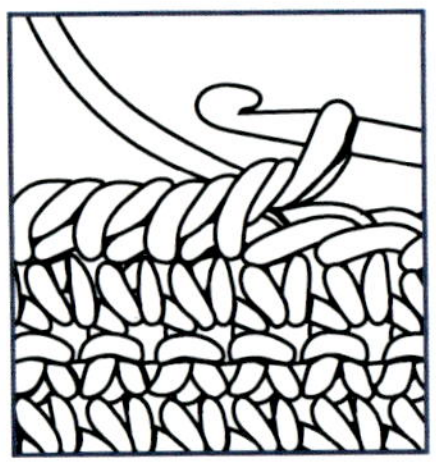

WHIPSTITCH

With **wrong** sides together, sew through both pieces once to secure the beginning of the seam, leaving an ample yarn end to weave in later. Insert the needle from **front** to **back** through both strands on each piece ***(Fig. 9)***. Bring the needle around and insert it from **front** to **back** through the next strands on both pieces. Repeat along the edge, being careful to match stitches.

Fig. 9

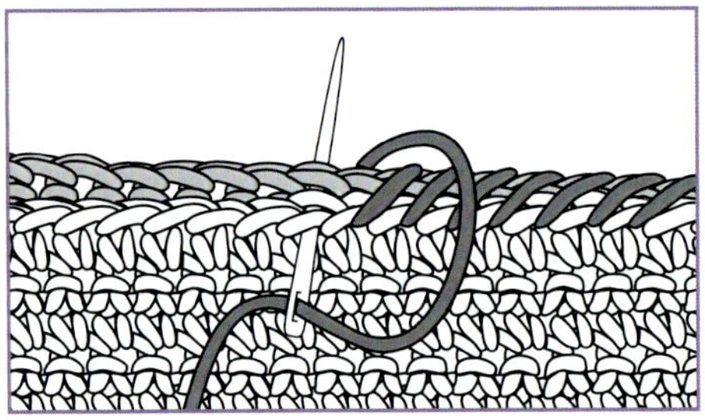

TASSEL

Cut a piece of cardboard 3" (7.5 cm) wide and as long as you want your finished tassel to be. Wind a double strand of yarn around the cardboard approximately 12 times. Cut an 18" (45.5 cm) length of yarn and insert it under all of the strands at the top of the cardboard; pull up **tightly** and tie securely. Leave the yarn ends long enough to attach the tassel.

Cut the yarn at the opposite end of the cardboard and then remove it ***(Fig. 10a)***. Cut a 12" (30.5 cm) length of yarn and wrap it **tightly** around the tassel, 1" (2.5 cm) below the top ***(Fig. 10b)***; tie securely. Trim the ends.

Fig. 10a

Fig. 10b

TWISTED CORD

Cut two pieces of yarn, each four times longer than the finished length for the Twisted Cord. Holding all four pieces together, fasten one end to a stationary object **or** have another person hold it; twist until **tight**. Fold in half and let it twist itself; knot the ends and trim to 2" (5 cm).

Each project in this leaflet was made using Medium Weight Yarn. Any brand of Medium Weight Yarn may be used. It is best to refer to the yardage/meters when determining how many balls or skeins to purchase. Remember, to arrive at the finished size, it is the GAUGE/TENSION that is important, not the brand of yarn.

For your convenience, listed below are the specific yarns used to create our photography models.

yarn INFORMATION

BABY'S FAVORITE BLANKIE
Version A
TLC® Essentials™
Green - #2615 Lt Celery
Blue - #2821 Paradise Blue
Off-White - #2313 Aran
Version B
Caron® Simply Soft®
Variegated - #2712 Baby Brights Ombre
Yellow - #2613 Soft Yellow
Lavender - #2664 Orchid

MAKE WAVES HAT
Caron® Simply Soft®
Dark Blue - #2626 Country Blue
Lt Blue - #2624 Lt Country Blue
White - #2601 White

BIRTHDAY CAKE CAP
Caron® Simply Soft®
Variegated - #2712 Baby Brights Ombre
Yellow - #2613 Soft Yellow

LITTLE GUY PREEMIE CAP
TLC® Essentials™
Green - #2615 Lt Celery
Blue - #2821 Paradise Blue

YOUR WAY SCARF AND CLOCHE SET
Version A
Red Heart® Super Saver®
Tan - #4313 Aran Fleck
TLC® Essentials™
Black - #2112 Black
Version B
TLC® Essentials™
Green - #2673 Med Thyme
Orange - #2254 Persimmon
Red - #2913 Ranch Red

FESTIVE HAT
Red Heart® Kids™
Variegated - #2935 Sherbet
Green - #2652 Lime

L'IL LUMBERJACK CAP
TLC® Essentials™
Brown - #2335 Taupe
Red Heart® Super Saver®
Tan - #4313 Aran Fleck

EASY BREEZY HAT
Caron® Simply Soft® Shadows
#0006 Dark Moss

TIED UP TOPPER
Bernat® Denim Style
Variegated - #03108 Indigo
TLC® Essentials™
Off-White - #2313 Aran

TRI CORNER CAP
Lion Brand® Wool-Ease®
Tan - #402 Wheat
Maroon - #138 Cranberry
Green - #180 Forest Green Heather
Blue - 115 Blue Mist

ELF CAP
Red Heart® Super Saver®
#4313 Aran Fleck

TWO TASSELS, NO HASSLES HAT
Caron® Simply Soft®
Black - #2680 Black
Grey - #2710 Grey Heather
Maroon - #2721 Autumn Red

production TEAM

Instructional Editor - Sarah J. Green
Technical Editor - Joan Beebe
Editorial Writer - Susan McManus Johnson
Graphic Artist - Amy Gerke
Senior Graphic Artist - Lora Puls
Photo Stylist - Michelle Uhiren
Photographers - Jason Masters and Kyle McLaughlin